DOLLS & TOYS

COMPILED BY TONY CURTIS

All prices quoted in this book are obtained from a variety
of auctions in various countries and are converted to dol-
lars at the rate of exchange prevalent at the time of sale.

ISBN   0-86248-009-4

Copyright © Lyle Publications MCMLXXXI
Published by Lyle Publications, Glenmayne, Galashiels, Selkirkshire, Scotland.

INTRODUCTION

This book is one of a series specially devised to aid the busy professional dealer in his everyday trading. It will also prove to be of great value to all collectors and those with goods to sell, for it is crammed with illustrations, brief descriptions and valuations of hundreds of antiques.

Every effort has been made to ensure that each specialised volume contains the widest possible variety of goods in its particular category though the greatest emphasis is placed on the middle bracket of trade goods rather than on those once-in-a-lifetime museum pieces whose values are of academic rather than practical interest to the vast majority of dealers and collectors.

This policy has been followed as a direct consequence of requests from dealers who sensibly realise that, no matter how comprehensive their knowledge, there is always a need for reliable, up-to-date reference works for identification and valuation purposes.

When using your Antiques and their Values Book to assess the worth of goods, please bear in mind that it would be impossible to place upon any item a precise value which would hold good under all circumstances. No antique has an exactly calculable value; its price is always the result of a compromise reached between buyer and seller, and questions of condition, local demand and the business acumen of the parties involved in a sale are all factors which affect the assessment of an object's 'worth' in terms of hard cash.

In the final analysis, however, such factors cancel out when large numbers of sales are taken into account by an experienced valuer, and it is possible to arrive at a surprisingly accurate assessment of current values of antiques; an assessment which may be taken confidently to be a fair indication of the worth of an object and which provides a reliable basis for negotiation.

Throughout this book, objects are grouped under category headings and, to expedite reference, they progress in price order within their own categories. Where the description states 'one of a pair' the value given is that for the pair sold as such.

The publishers wish to express their sincere thanks
to the following for their kind help and assistance
in the production of this volume:

JANICE MONCRIEFF
NICOLA PARK
CARMEN MILIVOYEVICH
ELAINE HARLAND
MAY MUTCH
MARGOT RUTHERFORD
JENNIFER KNOX

Printed by Apollo Press, Worthing, Sussex, England.
Bound by R. J. Acford, Chichester, Sussex, England.

CONTENTS

AIRCRAFT

Non-flying model of a Bristol
Fighter, 31.5cm. wingspan.
$100 £45

Meccano bi-plane construction kit, circa 1933,
1ft.3in. long. $112 £50

Dinky Mayo composite aircraft.
$135 £60

A non-flying scale model of a bi-plane.
$225 £100

A metal scale model of the Nazi airship
Hindenburg, 24in. long, by Marklin.
$350 £155

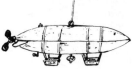

Lehmann EII tinplate zeppelin,
circa 1912, 7¾in. long.
$370 £165

Model of the Bristol Scout type C, 1915.
$405 £180

German clockwork airship toy.
$560 £250

Bryan's 'The Clock' amusement machine, circa 1952, 2ft.9in. high. $100 £45

Bryan's 'Hidden Treasure' penny-in-the-slot amusement machine, 70cm. high. $112 £50

Fireworks reward amusement machine, circa 1933, 2ft.8in. high. $125 £55

Conveyor amusement machine, 3ft. high, 1945-50. $145 £65

Gottlieb World's Fair pin-ball machine, circa 1963, 4ft.3½in. long. $305 £135

Silver screen one-reel bandit by Tom Boland, Leeds, circa 1945-50. $305 £135

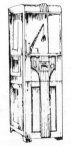

American merchantman crane amusement machine by Exhibit Supply Co., circa 1960. $495 £220

English 'Peerless' ghost story penny-in-the-slot amusement machine, circa 1950, 68in. high. $495 £220

Ahrens automatic palmistry amusement machine, 193cm. high. $730 £325

AUTOMATONS

Late 19th century American cold painted cast iron 'Black Boy' timepiece, 1ft.3½in. high. $335 £150

Early 20th century seascape automaton under a glass dome, 1ft.3in. high. $630 £280

Late 19th century French musical seascape automaton, 2ft.4in. high. $865 £385

Mid 19th century musical automaton, 20in. high. $880 £390

Tea party musical automaton, German, circa 1914, 11½in. wide. $1,125 £500

Late 19th century French musical seascape automaton, 1ft.8in. high. $1,295 £575

An early 19th century automaton clock, signed on back plate Pepin a Paris, 22in. high. $1,800 £800

A French presentation timepiece automaton by Cooke & Knelvey, Paris, 1ft.7in. high. $1,910 £850

A levitation automaton depicting Snow White lying on a couch, 45in. x 38in., circa 1920. $2,250 £1,000

10

A German itinerant clock-maker figure, carrying a clock on his chest, 13¾in. high, late 18th century.
$2,250 £1,000

Late 19th century French composition headed musical automaton.
$2,475 £1,100

A Charles X ormolu mantel clock, 37cm. high.
$2,700 £1,200

An automaton figure 'The Photographer'.
$2,815 £1,250

A French gilt metal clock automaton stamped on the back plate H.L., circa 1900. $3,600 £1,600

A fine 19th century French automaton group.
$4,500 £2,000

Late 19th century French musical automaton, 'The Hunter at Rest', 2ft.3in.
$4,950 £2,200

A late 19th century French magician's 'Cups and Balls' clock automaton, signed P. Garnier, Paris, 1ft.9in. high.
$4,950 £2,200

Automaton clock, Augsburg 1627.
$36,000 £16,000

11

AUTOMATONS
ANIMALS

Grizzly bear automaton who moves his legs and bends forward. $325 £145

An amusing English cat tea party automaton, the cardboard construction operated by a clockwork mechanism at the rear. $450 £200

A French monkey automaton who rises from a papier mache pineapple to music, circa 1898. $790 £350

Late 19th century French monkey drummer automaton, 1ft.6in. high. $865 £385

Late 19th century French musical rabbit automaton, 9in. high. $970 £430

Late 19th century French musical rabbit automaton, 8in. high. $1,315 £585

Mid 19th century French monkey trio barrel organ automaton, 3ft. high. $5,625 £2,500

Late 19th century monkey musician trio automaton, 1ft.1in. high. $5,850 £2,600

Musical piggy duo automaton, 1ft.3in. high, French. $8,100 £3,600

19th century singing bird box.
$900 £400

Two singing birds in a brass
cage. $700 £310

An early 19th century singing bird in a brass cage.
$925 £410

Late 19th century French
singing bird automaton, 1ft.
9in. high. $1,125 £500

Swiss enamel singing bird
box. $1,125 £500

19th century French gilt
brass bird automaton.
$1,315 £585

French nightingale singing
bird automaton, 1ft.9½in.
high, circa 1900.
$1,610 £715

Late 19th century French
singing birds automaton,
1ft.10in. high.
$1,755 £780

Late 19th century French
singing bird automaton,
17in. high. $1,855 £825

AUTOMATONS
CLOWNS

Early 20th century French musical automaton group of three clowns, 1ft.4in. high.　$620 £275

Late 19th century French clown and horse musical automaton, 1ft.2½in. wide. $790 £350

A late 19th century juggling clown automaton, 2ft. 5in. high.　$1,350 £600

A French musician automaton, the figure with composition head, wearing a scarlet long-tailed coat, circa 1900, 1ft.11in. high. $2,025 £900

A French musical automaton, circa 1900, 1ft.2in. high.　$1,350 £600

19th century clown with dancing midget, musical box inside. $1,800 £800

19th century French musical automaton.
$4,500 £2,000

Pierrot serenading the Moon, late 19th century automaton, 20in. high.　$5,625 £2,500

Late 19th century French Jumeau smoking doll automaton, 2ft. high.
$5,850 £2,600

14

DANCERS

AUTOMATONS

Late 19th century American clockwork dancing doll toy, 9¾in. high. $395 £175

Mid 19th century English dancing dolls toy, 10½in. high. $395 £175

An American National microphone dancer, 1ft.1in. high, circa 1935. $450 £200

Victorian automaton of an Indian dancer. $1,800 £800

Spanish dancer automaton who taps her foot, rotates and shakes her tambourine. $2,475 £1,100

Late 19th century French musical ballerina automaton, 1ft.10in. high. $2,700 £1,200

Musical automaton by E. Jumeau, 21in. high. $2,810 £1,250

Early 20th century French dancing girl automaton, the bisque headed doll with glass eyes, 1ft.10in. high. $2,810 £1,250

An animated snake dancer with a musical movement by Decamps of Paris. $5,175 £2,300

15

AUTOMATON FIGURES
DOLLS

19th century musical box, surmounted by a mechanical figure of a woman, 1ft.6in. high. $675 £300

Late 19th century French smoking doll automaton, 1ft.9in. high.$900 £400

An electrically operated mechanical tea advertisement, in the form of a lady with a teapot and cup, 36in. high. $900 £400

An early 20th century French sleeping doll automaton, 1ft. 2in. wide. $1,575 £700

Early 20th century German flower girl automaton, 1ft. 8in. high. $2,250 £1,000

A 19th century bisque headed automaton doll. $2,475 £1,100

Composition headed automaton figure of a Japanese woman. $4,050 £1,800

Doll automaton with bisque head and shoulders, circa 1860-80, 2ft.2in. high. $6,975 £3,100

'Screaming' Jumeau bisque headed musical automaton doll. $10,690 £4,750

MUSICIANS

Late 19th century French negro accordion player musical automaton, 11½in. high. $790 £350

Early 20th century French musical trio automaton, 1ft.10in. wide. $790 £350

19th century musical doll automaton. $980 £435

17in. doll, whose head moves as her hands play the piano, which is really a musical box. $1,675 £745

English barrel organ grinder automaton, circa 1920, 2ft.2in. high. $1,855 £825

A late 19th century French musician automaton, 1ft. 10in. wide. $2,475 £1,100

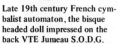

Late 19th century French cymbalist automaton, the bisque headed doll impressed on the back VTE Jumeau S.O.D.G. $2,925 £1,300

A French musical pianist automaton with makers plaque G. Vichy Fils, 1ft. 3in. wide, circa 1900. $2,980 £1,325

A French automaton of a negro musician from the third quarter of the 19th century, 3ft. high. $5,060 £2,250

17

BUSES

A wooden model of a red London bus. $160 £70

Charles Rossignol clockwork Paris bus, 12in. long. $180 £80

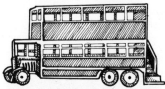 

Old London 1925 double-decker omnibus, 22in. long by 12½in. high, with light-up lamps. $250 £110

A Chad Valley clockwork biscuit tin, 1947, 10in. long. $270 £120

A tinplate trolley bus, French, circa 1905, 11in. long. $450 £200

Gunthermann clockwork tram, circa 1920, 9½in. long. $475 £210

A Toonerville Trolley by Fischer & Co., Germany, 13cm. long. $620 £275

A Georges Carette clockwork omnibus, 1ft. 1in. wide. $1,410 £625

Arnold Tin Lizzy toy car, German, 1950's, with box. $55 £25

Painted tin clockwork motor car with the driver holding a balloon, 6in. long. $80 £35

Structo clockwork racing car, 31cm. long. $108 £48

One of a set of four army vehicles and artillery. $115 £50

Royal Air Mail Service car by Dinky, slightly worn. $135 £60

Schuco Lady sports car, German, 1951, 9in. long. $135 £60

A Line's Bros. clockwork open sports car with front wheeled steering, 1ft.4in. long. $135 £60

Clockwork 'Old Shaker Car', Japan 1936, with flashing headlights, 11in. long. $135 £60

CARS

Schuco Police Patrol car, German, 1952, 8in. long. $145 £65

A Lehmann's clockwork 'Also' car, circa 1930, 4in. long.
$170 £75

Rossignol clockwork taxi and driver, 14cm. long, French. $170 £75

Clockwork 'Home James', English, 1900, 4in. high. $190 £85

Battery driven model of a 1925 vintage car. $200 £90

Lehmann automobile and driver.
$200 £90

Pre-war Marklin Auto Union Record car.
$200 £90

1920's clockwork Bing Model T Ford, painted black, 16cm. long. $215 £95

20

A Moko clockwork six cylinder saloon, 9½in. long. $225 £100

A. W. Butcher, London, model 'Primus Motor Chassis' construction, 13in. long, circa 1930. $225 £100

'Bluebird', 1935, made by Britain's Ltd., England. $250 £110

Late 19th century friction toy car, 12in. long. $340 £150

French hand enamelled tinplate clockwork sedan, circa 1904, 14in. long. $370 £165

Meccano motor car construction set No. 2, complete with driver, instruction sheet, key etc. $385 £170

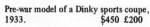

Jonet Francais tin model of an Alfa Romeo racing car. $450 £200

Pre-war model of a Dinky sports coupe, 1933. $450 £200

CARS

Hess friction drive limousine, 8¼in. long, circa 1920-25. $485 £210

Hessmobile car, clockwork. $470 £210

Tinplate double garage and two cars, 1920's. $495 £220

Bing open tourer, German, circa 1918, 11½in. long. $495 £220

Pre-war Dinky model of an open two-seater car, 1933-35. $540 £240

Rare 1930's model of a police car by Britain, in original box. $540 £240

Lehmann 'tut-tut' tinplate motor car, circa 1910, 6¾in. long. $550 £245

Model of 'The Railton New Wonder Car'. $565 £250

Chad Valley clockwork saloon, circa 1947. $745 £330

Clockwork Gunthermann saloon, 14½in. long, circa 1925. $870 £385

Lehmann tinplate clockwork model 'Auto UHU' in original box. $945 £420

Bing clockwork tinplate two-seater Mercedes, 9½in. long, circa 1912. $1,295 £575

Bing tinplate car with rubber tyres, circa 1903. $1,465 £650

Doll & Co. four-seater spirit-fired tourer, German, 1920. $2,475 £1,100

Scale model Bentley, 14in. long. $2,815 £1,250

A tinplate clockwork landaulette by Georges Carette, about 1910. $2,925 £1 300

23

CARTS & CARRIAGES

Child's red and blue toy pony cart.
$115 £50

Hand built and painted model of a London carriage with two open passenger seats, 1ft.1in. wide.
$225 £100

Hand built and painted model of an open Landau with folding hoods, cushioned seats and hinged doors, 1ft.2in. wide. $280 £125

Miniature Hansom cab with rubber tyred wheels and opening doors.
$295 £130

Scale model of a Northant's spindle-sided wagon. $340 £150

A 19th century model of an open carriage. $360 £160

A hand built and hand painted model of the London-York Royal Mail coach, 1ft.3in. wide.
$360 £160

Beautifully made miniature milk float.
$385 £170

Scale model of a pony trap with original coach painted woodwork in blue and green with yellow lines, circa 1830, 19in. long. $405 £180

Mid 19th century goat and dog cart for a child, complete with leather harness, 20in. wide, 68in. overall. $550 £245

Scale model of a yellow and black Hansom horse drawn cab. $550 £245

Child's Victorian Shetland pony trap painted in deep crimson, with black upholstery, brass studs and two brass V.R. escutcheons, 40in. high, 32in. wide, 77in. overall. $620 £275

Late 19th century model of a Lord Mayor's coach, 23in. long. $620 £275

A model of a 19th century trap. $620 £275

Sicilian miniature cart, carved and painted, 5ft.1in. long. $1,070 £475

A 19th century model of a steam horseless carriage compound, 11½in. long. $2,475 £1,100

COMMERCIAL VEHICLES

Part of a lot of thirteen lorries and transporters by Dinky. $45 £20

Part of a lot of eleven service vehicles by Dinky, circa 1937-60.
$55 £25

Builders and Merchants truck, made by Triang in 1951, 9in. long. $55 £25

Part of a lot of six Dinky buses, circa 1937-60. $55 £25

Regulation tyre limber, boxed, and a Britain's Beetle lorry with driver, boxed. $60 £26

One of a collection of twenty-six agricultural, construction and army vehicles by Dinky. $80 £35

Toy Bentalls removal van. $125 £55

Army wagon with soldiers and despatch rider, made in Japan, 1920. $135 £60

Wells clockwork B.P. motor delivery lorry, circa 1935, 6½in. long. $135 £60

Clockwork charabanc caravan, made by Minic in 1920, fully furnished inside, 14in. long. $135 £60

A model of a Royal Mail van of the 1920's period, 11¼in. high. $170 £75

Lehmann's clock work delivery van, circa 1910, 18in. long. $190 £85

Rare Edwardian Macfarlane Lang & Co.'s tinplate biscuit tin, with hinged roof, 19.5cm. long. $205 £90

A tin Lyons 1910 open delivery van. $205 £90

Part of a lot of eight commercial vans and lorries by Dinky. $225 £100

Dinky model of a Holland Coachcraft van No. 31. $225 £100

COMMERCIAL VEHICLES

A Lehmann's clockwork truck, circa 1910, 7in. long. $250 £110

Rare model of an International Stores biscuit tin, 32cm. long. $250 £110

Gun mounted on a tank chassis by Britain. $260 £115

Dinky super toy Weetabix Guy van, No. 514, in cardboard box, 5¾in. long. $305 £135

A scale model of a 1910 delivery van, 87cm. long. $350 £155

Dinky 28a Type 1 square yellow van. $540 £240

One of a collection of five commercial vehicles by Dinky. $1,800 £800

Lehmann Royal Mail 585 tinplate delivery van. $2,250 £1,000

German doll by Armand
Marseille. $170 £75

A bisque headed baby doll,
marked AM351/3K, 12in.
                    $170 £75

Bisque porcelain headed doll
by Armand Marseille, Ger-
many, 12in. high. $215 £95

German porcelain headed
baby doll by Armand
Marseille, 60cm. high.
                    $225 £100

Armand Marseille bisque
headed doll, 17in. high.
                    $225 £100

German bisque porcelain
baby doll impressed A.M.
                    $250 £110

A brown bisque baby doll
with sleeping eyes and
closed mouth, on brown
bent-limb baby's body,
13½in. tall, marked A.M.
341/3½K. $250 £110

German doll with kid body
made by Armand Marseille,
1900, 20in. tall.$280 £125

Armand Marseille negro bisque headed baby doll, 19in.
high. $295 £130

29

DOLLS
AMERICAN

American Ives & Co. clock-work walking doll, circa 1880, 9½in. high.
$845 £375

American Ives & Co., clock-work walking doll, circa 1880, 9½in. high.
$560 £250

American Ives & Co. clock-work walking doll, 9½in. high, circa 1880.
$900 £400

BATHING BELLE

Bisque bathing belle with blue and white suit and turquoise bathing cap, 6in. long. $80 £35

German bisque bathing beauty, 7in. tall.
$100 £45

All bisque 'Nudie' of fine quality, with mohair wig, 6in. long. $145 £65

BEBE BRU

Bisque headed Bebe doll.
$1,800 £800

Bisque headed Bebe doll, 10in. high. $2,810 £1,250

Bru Jne 4 doll, 12½in. high. $3,555 £1,580

French bisque Bru doll with paperweight eyes and kid body, 22in. tall.
$3,940 £1,750

Bebe Bru doll with paperweight eyes and swivel head.
$4,950 £2,200

Bisque headed Bebe Bru with original clothes.
$5,175 £2,300

A rare two-faced doll by Brue with original clothes.
$7,310 £3,250

French bisque headed doll by Brue, marked Bebe Bru No. 7.
$7,310 £3,250

Bisque headed Bebe doll by Bru, Paris, 24in. high.
$11,250 £5,000

19th century French bisque doll by Brue.
$13,500 £6,000

French Bru doll with original clothes.
$15,750 £7,000

Brue leather bodied doll, head, arms and bust of porcelain, 25½in. high.
$18,000 £8,000

DOLLS
DOLL'S HOUSE

Doll's house boy doll, 3½in. tall, circa 1860. $70 £30

Doll's house lady doll, 6in. tall, circa 1860. $70 £30

Bisque headed doll's house doll, 5in. tall. $80 £35

Doll's house doll of a man, 7in. high, circa 1860. $100 £45

Grandpa doll's house doll, 5½in. high. $115 £50

Grandma doll's house doll, 5¾in. tall. $115 £50

Bisque doll's house doll, 5in. tall. $125 £55

Model of the Dionne quintuplets, 1934, 7.5cm. tall. $270 £120

Rare mid 19th century bisque 'frozen Charlotte' doll, 5½in. tall. $595 £265

32

17th century style court
doll in Elizabethan dress,
with clay head and hands,
stuffed body, wearing
period jewellery.
$385 £170

19th century carved wood
figure of a cobbler.
$170 £75

Art Deco carved walnut
standing figure of a nude
girl, stamped N.J. Forrest,
1926. $170 £75

Japanese festival doll of a
mounted Samurai warrior.
$395 £175

Early 19th century pedlar
doll by C. & H. White,
Milton, Portsmouth, 9in.
high. $510 £225

Early 19th century model
of a town crier. $540 £240

Pedlar doll with papier
mache head and moul-
ded hair, 8in. high,
circa 1840.$675 £300

Three Martha Thompson bisque
portrait models of The Queen,
Prince Charles and Princess
Anne. $675 £300

One of a pair of early 19th
century pedlar dolls by C.
& H. White, Milton, Portsmouth, 9in. high.
$1,080 £480

A French cloth doll, 1920's, label marked 'Poupees Gerbs', 2ft.4½in. high. $45 £20

One of two unusual cloth dolls, French, 1920's, 2ft. 10in. high. $65 £30

One of three French cloth dolls, 1920's, one 2ft.6in. high. $80 £35

One of two French cloth dolls, 1920's, 2ft.4½in. tall. $125 £55

Small 19th century French doll with a porcelain head. $180 £80

A bisque headed child doll with jointed composition body, marked S.F.B.J. Paris 10, 23½in. tall. $250 £110

A bisque headed child doll dressed in red, marked Dep 11, 25½in. tall. $280 £125

A bisque headed child doll with jointed composition body, marked Unis France 71 149 301, 23in. tall. $280 £125

Victorian doll impressed 'Fabrication Francaise al and Cie Limoges Cherie 5', 19in. high. $280 £125

A French bisque headed doll dressed in pink and white. $305 £135

A doll with bisque head and papier mache limbs and body, 29in. high. $325 £145

A French 'Bon Bon' doll with bisque head marked Gebruder Krauss, 20in. high. $450 £200

French bisque headed doll with kid body and bisque arms, 17in. tall. $675 £300

A French bisque headed doll, 18in. high. $730 £325

French porcelain headed doll with jointed limbs and sleeping eyes. $755 £335

A French porcelain headed doll, with jointed limbs. $755 £335

French bisque swivel headed doll with composition body and glass eyes, 20in. tall. $900 £400

A dignified 19th century French doll. $1,010 £450

DOLLS
FRENCH

Attractive French shoulder bisque doll, possibly by Huret, 17½in. tall.
$1,305 £580

Very rare paper doll marked La Poupee Modele with six dresses and three head dresses.
$1,305 £580

French bisque headed doll, marked F. G.$1,350 £600

Parisienne bisque headed doll with pale blue eyes.
$1,800 £800

Fine mid 19th century French bisque doll, possibly by Huret, circa 1860, with various items of clothing. $2,205 £980

A French doll stamped Mme. Rohmer with a swivel china head.
$2,250 £1,000

Huret bisque doll, 17in. high, hands and body repaired, marked Paris 1867. $2,430 £1,050

Early 20th century bisque headed clockwork walking doll in original clothes and box. $4,050 £1,800

Fine French socketed bisque fashion doll, circa 1860, 18in. high.
$4,500 £2,000

A metal headed doll with moulded and painted hair, the stuffed body with wooden arms, marked Germany 5, 16in. tall.
$115 £50

German doll, circa 1890.
$135 £60

19th century German bisque headed doll.
$135 £60

German bisque shoulder headed doll with kid body. $145 £65

A celluloid headed child doll with fixed brown eyes and jointed composition body, marked K & W W298/12 with a turtle mark, 26½in. tall. $145 £65

A German sleeping doll with a bisque face. $170 £75

A German doll with bisque head and legs, and with head dress and clothes.
$180 £80

Sartorial German doll, made from an automaton.
$180 £80

19th century German bisque headed baby doll.
$225 £100

A German porcelain headed sleeping doll, 2ft. high.
$235 £105

German doll, 1920's, 24in. tall, head made by Heubach for Seyfarth and Reinhart.
$250 £110

19th century German bisque headed doll.
$260 £115

Max Handwerk German doll with bisque head and ball jointed limbs.
$270 £120

German Lehmann mechanical sailor, 7½in. high, circa 1912-14.
$270 £120

Bisque headed doll with composition body and limbs stamped Thuringa, Germany.
$270 £120

German porcelain headed talking doll, 60cm. high.
$270 £120

Ringmaster from the Schoenhut's Humpty Dumpty circus with bisque head, 9in. high. $280 £125

German doll made by Alt. Beck and Gottschalk, 1910, 26in. tall.
$280 £125

German bisque 'goo-goo' doll, 8in. high. $280 £125

Kesner lady doll with articulated arms and legs, 24in. tall. $295 £130

All wood doll with swivel head and painted eyes, marked Schoenhut, 17in. tall. $325 £145

German bisque china headed doll, 11in. high. $325 £145

19th century German bisque headed doll. $325 £145

German doll with sleeping brown eyes, in original box and clothes. $395 £175

Kathe Kruse girl doll with real hair wig, 20in. high. $395 £175

Bisque headed German doll with smiling face, in original clothes and box. $415 £185

Kathe Kruse wistful doll signed on foot in purple, 18in. high. $495 £220

39

DOLLS
GERMAN

Rare Biedermeier shoulder papier mache doll, 13in. high, circa 1825.
$640 £285

German shoulder papier mache doll, 11½in. high, circa 1840. $990 £440

German shoulder china head doll with kid body, 16in. high, circa 1870.
$1,125 £500

German shoulder china doll, 17¼in. high, circa 1860, with a baby.
$1,350 £600

Biedermeier shoulder papier mache doll, 21in. high, circa 1830.
$1,465 £650

Rare mid 19th century Motschmann articulated china doll, 10in. high.
$1,675 £745

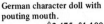

Steiner bisque doll, 19in. high, with white broderie anglaise dress.
$2,025 £900

German character doll with pouting mouth.
$2,475 £1,100

'Wendy' bisque doll by Bruno Schmidt of Waltershausen, circa 1900.
$4,275 £1,900

40

German, thirties type half doll with mohair wig, 4in. high. $55 £25

German thirties type china half doll, 4in. high.$70 £30

China half doll, 5in. high, with fine detail, no marks. $90 £40

China half doll of pale colouring except for oranges in the basket, 4in. high. $135 £60

French, late Victorian doll shaped rattle. $135 £60

China half doll, 4½in. high, with blue grey hair. $180 £80

Bisque half doll with the Goebel symbol, 4in. high. $190 £85

A bisque headed doll with fixed blue eyes, closed mouth, wearing sequins and silver lace streamers, 14in. high. $235 £105

A musical jester doll with bisque head, wearing original clothes. $250 £110

Heubach 'Bunny' doll with yellow tinted egg, 5½in. high. $115 £50

A bisque headed character baby with composition baby's body, wearing sailor smock, 22in., marked Heubach 342.9. $200 £90

Bisque swivel headed doll with brown eyes, marked Heubach. $295 £130

German bisque shoulder headed doll with blue eyes, marked Heubach, 12in. tall. $295 £130

German bisque swivel headed doll with composition jointed body, marked Heubach, 18in. tall. $340 £150

Heubach mechanical doll which rocks very smoothly. $450 £200

JUMEAU

A French doll with a porcelain head marked 'Depose tete Jumeau', 21in. high. $730 £325

Bisque swivel headed doll with stationary paperweight eyes, marked Jumeau, 18in. tall. $900 £400

Bisque swivel headed doll with glass eyes, marked Jumeau, 20in. tall. $900 £400

Jumeau bisque doll impressed Paris Fr.A.7, 15in. high. $955 £425

French doll impressed S.F.B.J., overstamped 'Tete Jumeau', body marked 'Bebe Jumeau' (1897), 24in. tall. $1,015 £450

Large Jumeau bisque doll, body marked 'Jumeau Diplome d'Honneur'. $1,215 £540

Jumeau open mouth doll with original wig, 1890, 23in. high. $1,630 £725

French Jumeau doll, 1890, 15in. high. $2,195 £975

19th century French bebe doll by Jumeau, 3ft. high. $2,700 £1,200

Jumeau phonograph doll. $3,940 £1,750

Rare brown bisque headed bebe Jumeau doll. $5,625 £2,500

20th century Jumeau doll with bisque head and body. $8,440 £3,750

43

DOLLS
KAMMER & REINHARDT

Kammer & Reinhardt celluloid character doll.
$225 £100

A character child doll with brown flirting eyes and bent-limb baby's body, marked K*R, 17in. high.
$280 £125

Kammer & Reinhardt 114 doll, 9in. tall, dressed in original clothes.
$1,240 £550

PARIAN

Dark-haired Parian doll with original dress, circa 1865, 11½in. long. $350 £155

Parian doll with moulded hair and blue eyes, circa 1870, 12in. high.
$440 £195

Parian doll with painted eyes and closed mouth, 21in. tall. $530 £235

Parian doll with cloth body, 14in. tall. $880 £390

Large Parian doll with fair hair and blue eyes, 24in. high. $955 £425

Dark-haired Parian doll, circa 1850. $990 £440

Schoenau & Hoffmeister doll with blue eyes, 26in. tall, circa 1909. $190 £85

Doll by Schoenau & Hoffmeister wearing a navy blue school gymslip. $190 £85

Large doll, impressed mark for Schoenau & Hoffmeister, 1909. $270 £120

Bisque china Schoenau Hoffmeister doll, circa 1905, 15in. tall. $295 £130

Schoenau & Hoffmeister doll, 25in. high, circa 1905. $340 £150

Schoenau & Hoffmeister doll, 21in. high. $2,700 £1,200

STEINER

German doll made by Herm. Steiner, 1912, 16in. long. $170 £75

Bisque swivel headed doll with glass eyes and pierced ears, marked Steiner. $340 £150

Fine Steiner bisque doll, circa 1880, 21in. high. $1,285 £570

45

Doll made by Simon & Halbig, circa 1905. $250 £110

A late Victorian Simon & Halbig doll, 28in. high. $280 £125

Simon & Halbig bisque headed doll with composite body, 94cm. long. $315 £140

Simon & Halbig, Kammer and Reinhardt doll, circa 1905. $450 £200

Bisque headed walking doll by Simon & Halbig, 42cm. high, with composition body. $945 £420

A bisque headed character doll by Simon & Halbig. $1,575 £700

19th century bisque headed doll by Simon & Halbig, 22in. high. $2,080 £925

Simon & Halbig Japanese character doll. $2,475 £1,100

Early 20th century 'Googly' doll by Simon & Halbig. $5,065 £2,250

46

Small bisque headed doll with stuffed body and composition arms, 26cm. long. $80 £35

Italian Lanci felt doll, 1930's. $115 £50

Late 19th century coloured doll with black high heeled boots. $115 £50

Bisque headed doll with painted blue eyes, circa 1875. $145 £65

Victorian china doll, 18in. high. $170 £75

Small Victorian doll with the original clothes. $180 £80

A Victorian bisque headed doll, in full national costume. $190 £85

Victorian doll with original clothing. $190 £85

Character baby doll marked W. Weyh, with blue eyes and closed mouth, 11in. high. $250 £110

China headed gentleman
doll, 16in. high.
$270 £120

Victorian bisque doll with
fixed blue eyes, 14in. tall.
$280 £125

Bisque headed doll with glass
eyes, circa 1875, 10½in. long.
$295 £130

'Little Nurse' from the Boer
War in original condition,
with fixed blue eyes.
$295 £130

19th century bisque head
mechanical doll in cane
chair, 23.5cm. high.
$340 £150

A composition shoulder
headed doll, with inset enamel eyes, cloth arms and
wooden body, circa 1845,
15½in. high. $340 £150

Lady doll with painted blue
eyes and brown brows,
circa 1890, 16½in. tall.
$340 £150

Bisque headed lady doll,
circa 1870, 11½in. tall.
$350 £155

Army doll from the 1914-
18 War period. $350 £155

Edwardian doll in original clothing, 15in. high. $450 £200

Victorian doll complete with carriage. $450 £200

Good Pierotti type shoulder wax doll, 10½in. high, circa 1875. $450 £200

Painted felt rag doll. $520 £230

Victorian doll with fine original clothes. $530 £235

Montanari poured shoulder wax doll, 23in. high, circa 1860. $595 £265

Shoulder bisque headed doll, 19in. high, circa 1880, with blonde wig. $595 £265

A muslin frocked doll with a wool wig, bisque arms and unjointed kid body. $620 £275

A china headed doll with stuffed cloth body, the kid hands with separated fingers, 31in. high. $730 £325

A china headed clockwork walking doll, gliding on three wheels in the base, 8½in. high. $790 £350

Bisque head and shoulder dancing doll, 18in. high. $845 £375

Grass stuffed Athabascan doll made of buckskin and decorated with trade beads, 17in. high. $1,240 £550

Bisque headed doll, 'Lucy', 100cm. high, with ball jointed limbs. $1,240 £550

Bisque character-headed boy doll. $1,350 £600

Lady Victoria Rose bisque head and shoulder portrait doll. $1,800 £800

Bisque headed character doll. $2,025 £900

50

Bisque headed character child doll. $2,700 £1,200

Bisque shoulder headed 'googly-eyed' doll with long velvet body. $3,940 £1,750

Victorian doll with wax covered face. $80 £35

A wax over composition doll with Motcham type floreated hands and feet, 15in. $100 £45

Wax head doll, brown eyes, blonde hair, 18in. high.
$125 £55

Wax doll with dress and shoes. $190 £85

A wax over composition doll, the cloth body with kid arms, the fingers separated, wearing a blue silk jacket and striped skirt, 25in. high. $260 £115

Late 19th century wax faced doll. $295 £130

Wax headed doll, 21½in. tall, circa 1880.
$340 £150

Poured wax doll stamped Frederic Aldis, 20in. high.
$630 £280

Wax two-faced doll stamped Deutsches Reichs-Patent U.S.P., circa 1870, 16in. high. $700 £310

DOLLS
WOOD

A carved wooden boy doll with painted hair and features, the body with wooden arms, 15½in.
$90 £40

American 19th century painted wooden doll, 29cm. high. $215 £95

One of three wooden peg dolls, 11½in. high, in late Victorian clothes.
$225 £100

An early carved limewood artist's articulated figure, 16in. high. $250 £110

Wooden swivel headed doll with glass eyes, 14in. tall.
$260 £115

A carved and painted wooden doll, the face with painted blue eyes and stitched brows, the stuffed body with wooden arms, circa 1860, 31in. high. $385 £170

A turned and carved wood doll's house doll wearing 19th century printed cotton dress, circa 1760, 9in. tall.
$980 £435

A George II painted wood doll, the face partly re-painted and fingers damaged, 22in. high. $1,315 £585

George III painted wooden doll, legs missing.
$1,910 £850

52

Carved and turned wooden
doll, early 19th century.
$2,475 £1,100

Carved painted wood
English baby doll, circa
1740. $2,815 £1,250

An excellent carved wooden
doll, circa 1740.
$3,825 £1,700

Queen Anne painted wood
doll, circa 1700, legs missing below knee.
$3,940 £1,750

George III carved and painted wooden doll, circa 1770.
$3,940 £1,750

Painted wooden doll, circa
1700, 10½in. high.
$3,940 £1,750

Carved and painted doll,
circa 1710.
$4,725 £2,100

Early turned and carved
wooden doll, circa 1780.
$5,400 £2,400

Pair of William and Mary
wooden dolls, 'Lord and
Lady Clapham'.
$45,000 £20,000

DOLLS' HOUSES

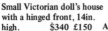

Small Victorian doll's house with a hinged front, 14in. high. $340 £150

A fine Victorian doll's house. $340 £150

Substantially built doll's house, with two reception rooms, hall, staircase, landing and two bedrooms. $395 £175

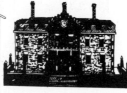

Victorian doll's house, 31in. wide. $395 £175

Late Georgian doll's house, 2ft.7in. wide. $450 £200

Doll's house dated circa 1912. $450 £200

Rare copper doll's house, named 'Shakespeare's House, Stratford-on-Avon' 13¾in. high. $450 £200

A large Triang toy doll's house, circa 1930, 3ft.8in. wide. $450 £200

Late 19th century doll's house. $510 £225

54

A well executed doll's house, made during World War II.
$565 £250

A doll's Victorian wooden house, of six rooms and a staircase, 119cm. wide.
$900 £400

Superb Victorian doll's house complete with miniature furniture.
$955 £425

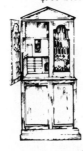

A doll's wooden house in the form of a three-storey building, with nine rooms.
$1,035 £460

Late Georgian stripped pine doll's house, 6ft.4in. high.
$1,125 £500

A large, painted, doll's wooden house, the lower section with outside staircase, 5ft.2in. high, 4ft. wide.
$1,125 £500

A Victorian doll's house with original furniture.
$1,125 £500

Rare Regency painted wooden two-storey doll's house and stand, 3ft.1in. wide.
$1,295 £575

Victorian doll's house, 2ft. 4in. high.
$1,295 £575

DOLLS' HOUSES

A fully furnished 19th century doll's house. $1,350 £600

A mid Victorian three-storey doll's house on stand, 3ft.5in. wide. $1,675 £745

Fully furnished Victorian doll's house. $1,800 £800

A late Victorian doll's house, 2ft.10in. wide. $2,025 £900

Hand-made model of a timber framed house. $2,025 £900

Victorian doll's house, completely fitted with furniture. $2,700 £1,200

Doll's wooden house, paper covered to simulate stone. $2,700 £1,200

Fine mid Victorian doll's house, fully furnished, 3ft. 9in. wide. $2,810 £1,250

Doll's house designed by Sir Wm. Clough Williams Ellis. $3,150 £1,400

German clockwork tinplate toy fire engine, 10in. long. $160 £70

Fire Rescue tender, French, 1933, ringing bell and extending ladder, 7in. long. $170 £75

A Tipp Co. clockwork fire engine, circa 1930, 1ft.7in. long. $280 £125

Early clockwork fire engine, made in Germany. $340 £150

Fine model of a horse-drawn fire engine, 15in. long. $340 £150

19th century model of a coal-fired horse-drawn steam fire engine, 14in. long, in a glass showcase. $1,715 £750

A working model of a Shand Mason horse-drawn fire engine, circa 1894. $3,375 £1,500

An exhibition class working model of a Merryweather steam fire engine built by Tyrer, Hastings. $10,125 £4,500

GAMES

Victorian child's wooden spinning top. $12 £5

Victorian child's wooden puzzle in box. $12 £5

Boxwood dice-cup. $34 £15

Chinese ivory cricket cage containing miniature dominoes, 2½in. high. $34 £15

Victorian child's snakes and ladders game, 16¾in. square. $40 £18

A Victorian abacus. $45 £20

Complete set of wooden skittles, circa 1875. $45 £20

Antique decorated wood 'Pope Joan' game, 10in. diam., circa 1870. $85 £38

American set of 'Snow White' picture bricks, circa 1946. $90 £40

French 'Jeu de Course' game, circa 1900, 10½ x 10½in. $102 £45

19th century Oriental carved wood games box. $112 £50

Mid Victorian child's shooting range. $112 £50

Fine boxed set of graduated pyramid and ABC picture blocks. $112 £50

Late 18th century Chinese ivory game of Bilboquet. $146 £65

1940's Mahjong set in carved wooden cabinet. $146 £65

Set of eleven coloured carpet bowls. $180 £80

Ivory and bamboo Mahjong set, circa 1910. $192 £85

An early Victorian folding backgammon board, made of walnut inlaid with rosewood, satinwood, boxwood and ebony, circa 1840. $192 £85

59

GAMES

19th century walnut roulette wheel inlaid with amboyna and kingwood.
$205 £90

Child's game 'Lamplough's Model Cricket'. $205 £90

French tinplate 'Jeu de Course', circa 1900, 18in. diam. $225 £100

Early 19th century lacquer games box with six lidded boxes and nine trays. $225 £100

Victorian walnut games box. $260 £115

Set of finely carved ivory Chinese puzzles in a gold and black lacquered box.
$335 £125

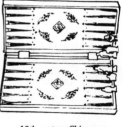

Victorian mahogany games box, circa 1880, including chess and dominoes.
$340 £150

English cast iron football game, circa 1910, 5ft. 6in. high. $495 £220

19th century Chinese export lacquer chess and backgammon board complete with ivory chessmen.
$530 £235

20th century sandalwood and ivory Indian games box, 18in. wide. $560 £250

Mid 19th century artist's paintbox, 1ft.10in. wide, English. $585 £260

19th century carved ivory chess set in a glazed case.
$620 £275

Mid Victorian compendium of games. $775 £345

An Ahrems test-your-strength machine, circa 1920, 6ft.7in. high.
$790 £350

Victorian coromandel wood games compendium in box, 13½in. wide. $1,125 £500

Goanese ivory chess and backgammon board.
$1,755 £780

English box and counters, 1755-1760, enamelled on copper, 6.5cm. wide.
$5,065 £2,250

Superb 17th century South German games table complete with games. $12,375 £5,500

61

HORSES

19th century child's toy horse. $145 £65

Victorian papier mache pull-along horse, circa 1870. $145 £65

Victorian, small carved wood horse on a stand. $145 £65

A Victorian child's carved wood toy horse, with pony hair mane and red leather bridle, 16½in. high. $180 £80

Child's pull-along horse covered with pony skin, circa 1850, 11½in. high. $215 £95

Mid Victorian hide covered pony, 18in. high, 17in. long. $280 £125

Victorian toy push horse with horse hair mane and leather bridle and saddle, 28in. high. $295 £130

A 19th century pair of carved wooden horses. $305 £135

A fine parchment covered toy pony on stand, with pull along wheeled base, circa 1860. $385 £170

Early 20th century wooden
horse with painted features.
$35 £15

Child's wooden rocking
horse with black hair
mane and tail and leat-
her bridle, reins and
stirrups. $260 £115

Small Victorian rocking
horse on oak stand,
29in. high. $305 £135

Late 19th century dapple
grey rocking horse on
fixed boat rockers.
$315 £140

A Victorian rocking
horse. $350 £155

A fine 19th century rock-
ing horse. $530 £235

Victorian rocking horse,
with no mane.
$550 £245

English carved and
painted rocking horse,
circa 1900, 7ft. long.
$745 £330

Late 17th century carved
and painted wood rock-
ing horse. $2,925 £1,300

Early 20th century painted tin horse and trap with Indian driver, 7in. long. $55 £25

1920 tin and wood pull-along toy.
                                    $80 £35

Victorian wooden model of a horse-drawn caravan, 28in. long.$180 £80

Carved giltwood model of a stage-coach with two horses, 56cm. wide. $180 £80

Early Victorian wooden pony and trap.
                                  $280 £125

A child's galloper tricycle, circa 1870, 3ft.4in. long. $305 £135

Tinplate clockwork horse and cart, by G. and K. Greppert & Keich, Brandenburg, 17cm. long.$325 £145

A cast iron cold painted model of a Hansom cab, 11in. long. $340 £150

Victorian child's wooden horse and cart. $340 £150

A wooden dray and pair with driver, 15in. high, 27½in. long, signed Gregory Ivory, 1892. $350 £155

A Lehmanns clockwork donkey and cart, circa 1910, 7½in. long. $495 £220

Toy horse and carriage made of papier mache and metal, circa 1890, 33cm. long. $575 £255

19th century carving of the London to Dorchester stagecoach. $575 £255

Late 19th century model of a horse drawn milkcart, 1ft.11in. long. $630 £280

Tsarist period peasant's carved wood model of a sleigh and three horses, circa 1840, 23in. long. $700 £310

Early 19th century child's three-wheeled carriage. $980 £435

LEAD FIGURES

Britain's model lead figure. $7 £3

Britain's set of Arabs on horseback. $34 £15

Two from a set of eight Britain's German Infantry, in original box. $45 £20

Britain's Somerset Light Infantry, 1905.
$45 £20

One of a set of eleven Britain's Cossacks, in original Whisstock box No. 136. $68 £30

A soldier of the 24th South Wales Borderers of the 1880's, wearing a pith helmet, 5¼in. high. $68 £30

Two from a set of fifteen Britain's United States Infantry, including one officer. $68 £30

A Napoleonic Grenadier of the Imperial Guard wearing a black bearskin with scarlet plume, 6½in. high.
$90 £40

A mounted figure of Henry, Duke of Lancaster, in full armour, by Ping. $100 £45

Royal Horse Artillery gun team with five outriders.
$100 £45

66

'Jack's Band' of ten musicians each seated on a gilt chair, with conductor, in original box. $100 £45

One of a set of sixteen Britain's Dublin Fusiliers, in original Whisstock box No. 109. $100 £45

Britain's set of French Legion Etrangere Infantry, with mounted officer.
                    $100 £45

One from a set of sixteen soldiers from Britain's Bulgarian Infantry, in box. $100 £45

Toy gun of the Royal Artillery with an officer and a team of gunners. $112 £50

One from a set of eight Britain's Danish Army Life Guards, in original box No. 2019. $112 £50

Royal Engineers pontoon section in original box No. 1254. $125 £55

Lead band of musicians. $125 £55

LEAD FIGURES

A model soldier by Robt.
Courtenay of Slough.
$135 £60

King's Royal Rifle Corps, lead soldiers by Britain.
$135 £60

A pre-1914 Britain's horse ambulance model. $145 £65

Set of nine lead soldiers of the band of
the 1st Lifeguards. $145 £65

Lead set of Snow White and
Seven Dwarfs by Britain,
1938. $145 £65

Lead model by Britain of pre-1914 Royal
Engineers. $160 £70

One of a set of sixteen
Britain's Italian Infantry
in Colonial Service dress.
$170 £75

Two from a set of sixteen Britain's Mexican Infantry in box, slightly damaged. $170 £75

Two from a set of ten Britain's Middlesex Yeomanry, dated 1903. $192 £85

Britain's model of the George IV coronation coach and horses, 20¼in. long. $215 £95

Part of a lot of twenty-eight mounted lead figures of the South Australian Lancers and First Lifeguards. $225 £100

Britain's model of a six-horse gun carriage. $225 £100

One from a set of Britain's Italian Carabinieri in original box, thirty-two pieces in all. $250 £110

LEAD FIGURES

Her Majesty's State coach drawn by eight horses, in original box.
$260 £115

Britain's Royal Horse Artillery team of lead soldiers. $260 £115

Set of Britain's Civilians, dated 1908, seven pieces in all. $270 £120

Britain's Royal Army Service wagon. $305 £135

Band of the Royal Horse Guards of twenty-five mounted figures and a few Beefeaters, contained in a Britain's box. $305 £135

Royal landau by Britain, 1953, with six horses. $330 £145

Set of Britain's South Australian Lancers in box. $340 £150

Part of a collection of late 19th century Ernest Heinrichsen flat lead figures.
$350 £155

LEAD FIGURES

Band of the U.S. Marine Corps, lead soldiers. $385 £170

Britain's South Australian Lancers, set of five in box, circa 1911. $385 £170

Heyde Roman display box. $450 £200

An American bridge building unit by Heyde, Germany. $470 £210

Set of four soldiers in original box.
$485 £215

Lead model of the landau of the Governor of the Punjab. $485 £215

Superb model of a 1914-18 gun unit. $540 £240

Set of Boer War supply column by Britain. $630 £280

73

LEAD FIGURES

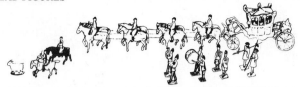

A Britain's complete boxed set of the Coronation display no. 1477, including Her Majesty's coronation stagecoach, 150 pieces. $630 £280

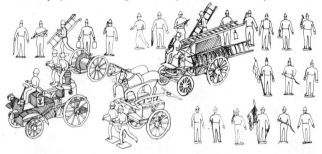

Part of a display of turn-of-the-century firefighters by Mignot, France. $870 £385

Part of a set of sixteen Britain's Salvation Army figures. $925 £410

Twenty-one man band of the Royal Marine Light Infantry. $2,140 £950

A pair of magical sand and sugar containers. $35 £15

Pair of turned wood magic tricks, circa 1910. $70 £30

An early sliding die box. $90 £40

A Will Goldston penetration frame in which a photograph is magically penetrated by a pencil, circa 1905. $115 £50

A bird cage canister, circa 1900. $125 £55

A large 'Head Chopper' once the property of the 'Great Levante', 4ft.4in. high. $170 £75

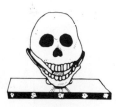

Collection of turned box-wood magic tricks, circa 1910. $170 £75

The 'Giant Bran Glass' trick in which the bran is transformed into a live dove, circa 1900. $200 £90

'The Talking Skull' which opens and closes its mouth at the will of the performer, circa 1920. $215 £95

Clockwork Steakhouse Joe, made in Japan. $70 £30

Clockwork Donald Duck by Schuco. $90 £40

Clockwork dancing Prince and Princess, 1936, 4½in. high. $100 £45

Louis Marx tinplate 'Ring-a-Ling' circus, 7½in. diam., circa 1930. $125 £55

Part of F. G. Taylor Zoo series, Chimpanzees' tea party eighteen-piece in original boxes. $170 £75

Marx clockwork walking Popeye, 8in. high. $180 £80

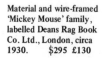

Clockwork 'Boy on a Swing', English 1937, 3½in. wide. $180 £80

German tinplate photographer toy, circa 1920, 5in. long. $250 £110

Material and wire-framed 'Mickey Mouse' family, labelled Deans Rag Book Co. Ltd., London, circa 1930. $295 £130

German tinplate clockwork 'Jolly Sambo', 6¾in. high, circa 1920. $305 £135

Mechanical rickshaw made by German firm of Lehmann, circa 1912. $340 £150

Victorian mechanical toy of a chef peeling a carrot. $340 £150

'Old Man Turning Windmill' made in German P.O.W. camp, 1917, figure cut out from old wood, 4in. long. $350 £155

Lehmann 'Wild West' bucking bronco tinplate toy, circa 1930, 6¼in. long. $416 £185

Hand enamelled clockwork toy, German, 1900, 6in. high. $430 £190

A Lehmann tinplate 'Walking down Broadway' couple, circa 1896, 6in. high. $745 £330

French painted tinplate clockwork bagatelle player, circa 1900. $745 £330

Early American tinplate Mickey Mouse clockwork toy, circa 1930. $1,125 £500

German tinplate clockwork fly, circa 1910. $95 £42

Tin mechanical toy bear, circa 1930, 6in. high. $100 £45

German tinplate clockwork beetle, circa 1900, 3¾in. long. $215 £95

A Lehmann mechanical flying bird, circa 1910, 7in. long. $250 £110

Mid 20th century clockwork cat, 1ft.3in. long. $250 £110

Climbing monkey, made in France, 1872, fully extended 4½in. $350 £155

Early 20th century French clockwork tiger, 1ft.11in. long. $395 £175

Fine G. G. Kellerman clockwork tinplate frog, German, circa 1930, 4¾in. high.$450 £200

Decamps mechanical ram, French, circa 1900, 1ft. 2in. long. $450 £200

Early 20th century German clockwork clown toy, 9in. high. $115 £50

Clockwork acrobatic clown, made in Germany. $55 £25

Schoenhut's crackerjack clown with original box and chair. $225 £100

German tinplate clockwork 'Jolly Clown', 6¾in. high, circa 1920. $225 £100

Victorian mechanical clown toy. $450 £200

Victorian dappled grey horse and clown toy. $450 £200

Old French toy walking clown, 1872, 9in. high. $530 £235

Coloured tinplate working model of a clown artist at work. $900 £400

German Phillip Vielmetter painted tin drawing clown, circa 1900, 5½in. high. $1,520 £675

1930's ice cream tricycle in good condition.
$90 £40

Unique Art 'Kiddy Cyclist' toy in tinplate, circa 1945-55, 8½in. wide. $115 £50

A child's Victorian automated toy of a polar bear on a tricycle.
$125 £55

A French toy in mahogany and glass case, circa 1900, 1ft.6in. wide.
$250 £110

German Arnold tinplate motorcycle, 8in. long, circa 1950. $250 £110

19th century wind-up toy depicting a young boy on a tricycle, 11in. wide, 9in. high.
$550 £245

Clockwork tinplate motorcycle, circa 1930, 8½in. long. $595 £265

Early French tricycle clockwork toy, circa 1870, 6¾in. long.
$865 £385

French clockwork tricyclist, circa 1870, with bisque head and original clothes. $1,170 £520

Japanese battery operated one-man band, by Alps.
$135 £60

Three little pigs, clockwork, by Schuco. $135 £60

Clockwork model, a 'Zilo-tone' by Wolverine Supply & Mfg. Co., circa 1930.
$385 £170

Tinplate clockwork 'Mickey Mouse' toy, German, circa 1930, 6¼in. long.
$395 £175

Marx clockwork mouse orchestra, 23cm. wide.
$450 £200

19th century French mech-anical toy soldier.
$520 £230

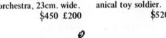

A French tinplate push-along drummer boy, circa 1890, 5¾in. high;
$595 £265

Distler clockwork organ grinder, circa 1923, German, 7in. high.
$1,025 £455

Mickey Mouse organ grin-der, about 1930, possibly by Distler, 6in. long.
$4,725 £2,100

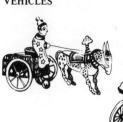

English tinplate novelty toy 'Banana Joe'. $20 £9

German clockwork toy, circa 1900. $80 £35

Lehmann bucking mule novelty toy in poor condition, with one leg missing, circa 1910. $80 £35

Louis Marx tinplate 'Goofy' toy, circa 1945, 8½in. long. $170 £75

A child's Victorian automated toy of three sailors on a painted wood carriage. $190 £85

Lehmann tinplate clockwork model 'The Bally Mule', in original box. $205 £90

Tinplate and clockwork clown in a cart by G. & K., 12.5cm. wide. $235 £105

Clockwork 'Man on a Wild Pig', German, 1882/86, 4½in. long. $260 £115

A wind-up Victorian toy complete with the original box. $350 £155

Clockwork 'Wheel of Death', Russian, 1896, 9in. high. $360 £160

Lehmann tinplate clockwork model, circa 1915. $385 £170

Coloured tinplate fly-wheel driven cock pulling a cart. $405 £180

A Lehmann's clockwork tricycle, circa 1910, 16.5cm. long. $430 £190

Lehmann tinplate clockwork model 'Naughty Boy', in original card box. $675 £300

Lehmann tinplate clockwork model 'Auto Sisters', in original card box. $765 £340

Coloured tinplate clockwork horseless carriage. $790 £350

Mechanical tinplate rickshaw by Lehmann, Germany, circa 1930, 7½in. long. $810 £360

German Lehmann 'anxious bride' clockwork toy, circa 1914, 8½in. long. $1,080 £480

MINIATURE FURNITURE

A miniature mahogany circular breakfast table, on pillar and block. $90 £40

Miniature 19th century rocking chair. $90 £40

19th century apprentice mahogany chest of drawers, 26cm. high. $135 £60

A miniature mahogany wardrobe, enclosed by two doors, with carved beaded borders, 16in. high, 13in. wide. $135 £60

Miniature Victorian mahogany sideboard with a mirrored back. $160 £70

Cast iron model cooking range, American, circa 1920, 1ft.1in. wide. $170 £75

Victorian half tester mahogany doll's bed, circa 1840. $280 £125

A miniature apprentice made settle, Brittany, circa 1850, in oak with hinged lid, 12¾in. long. $295 £130

Miniature 19th century piano decorated with marquetry, by W. A. Whittlesey, 14½in. wide. $340 £150

Child's tinplate cooking range, probably French, circa 1900, 18¼in. wide, complete with pans.
$360 £160

French walnut miniature child's bergere chair with carved fee. $385 £170

Working toy enamel range. $450 £200

A child's chair made of horns, 18in. high, circa 1820. $475 £210

Set of 19th century doll's mahogany furniture, bed 24in. long. $620 £275

Miniature 18th century Dutch oak armoire, 16¼in. high. $530 £235

Late 18th century Dutch miniature walnut cylinder bureau, circa 1770, 1ft.3in. high. $675 £300

Miniature mahogany long-case clock, 14in. high. $720 £320

Walnut and burr-walnut miniature bureau, 13¼in. high. $1,080 £480

Pair of small leather clogs with brass buckles. $22 £10

Late 19th century lace trimmed embroidered nightdress. $34 £15

Late 19th century child's wooden wheelbarrow, 3ft. long x 1ft.7in. wide. $67 £30

Art Deco teapot in the shape of a car. $67 £30

Doll's wooden teaset, circa 1870. $85 £38

Miniature record made for Queen Mary's dolls house. $100 £45

Victorian child's circular musical box with brass winding handle, 3in. diam., circa 1860. $108 £48

A push chair with cast iron frame with leaf suspension, English, 3ft.7in. long, mid 19th century. $145 £65

A Hollie Point baby's shirt and bonnet edged with Buckingham lace, 17th century. $195 £85

Rudge Whitworth tricycle with 5ft.5in. black frame, circa 1899. $250 £110

Late 19th century pair of unusual Anderson & Sons bicycle skates, 25in. long. $280 £125

Boy's riding jacket of brown worsted with blue satin waistcoat, circa 1785. $280 £125

Bingophone child's gramophone, circa 1925, German, turntable 17½in. diam. $350 £155

Miniature ruby glass tea service with gilt decoration, circa 1860. $475 £210

Scale model of a fairground organ. $1,350 £600

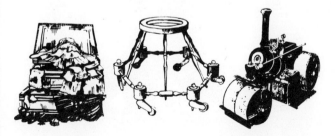

Trousseau for 19th century French Bru doll. $1,465 £650

A Charles II walnut baby walker. $2,475 £1,100

Scale model of a Waullis & Steevens 'Simplicity Roller', made in the late 20's. $3,375 £1,500

MODELS

A carved and pierced fretwork model of the frontage of Westminster Cathedral, in wood and glazed case, 3ft.6in. high.
$90 £40

A wooden model of a gypsy caravan, 14in. tall.
$115 £50

19th century model of a Royal Mail cart.
$190 £85

An early 19th century model of a sedan chair, 11in. high. $190 £85

19th century black painted wood and wire bird cage, 21in. long.
$190 £85

19th century model of a gypsy caravan.
$215 £95

Edwardian child's milk float, circa 1900, 12in. high.
$270 £120

A Victorian barking Boston terrier, 18in. long.
$280 £125

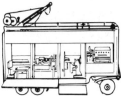

A well constructed six wheeled showman's
mobile workshop trailer, 2ft.2in. wide.
$350 £155

Self-propelled toy steam tricycle.
$450 £200

Two sections of a glass case containing
three scenes from 'Three Little Kittens',
58in. long. $585 £260

French sawmill model in a glass case.
$1,070 £475

Coin operated working model of Stephenson's
'Rocket' in glass case. $1,215 £540

Working model of a hand weaving
loom, circa 1900, English, 2ft.1½in.
high. $1,350 £600

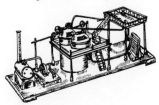

An early Bing tinplate model brewery, circa
1905, 1ft.7¾in. long. $2,080 £925

Early 19th century saddler's model
of a dapple grey stallion, 15.2 hands
high. $2,700 £1,200

MODEL BUILDINGS

19th century model of an English cottage made from oak. $135 £60

Shell model of 'Broughton Hall', 26 x 13in. $145 £65

Wooden fortress, circa 1950, sold with soldiers and animals. $145 £65

Austrian pre-World War I model Schloss. $160 £70

A wooden model of a railway signal box. $250 £110

A painted wood model of Noah's Ark, and a large collection of the carved wood animals and birds. $250 £110

Victorian model greengrocer's shop, 3½in. high, circa 1840. $340 £150

Toy stable, German, circa 1860, 2ft. 9in. wide. $395 £175

19th century model of Noah's Ark in carved wood complete with animals and Noah and his wife. $450 £200

A model of the 'Ancient House', Ipswich, circa 1920. $530 £235

A German toy castle made from hand painted pinewood, circa 1850, 19in. high. $620 £275

Mid 19th century Noah's Ark with 370 wooden animals, 56cm. long overall. $745 £330

Model of a Scottish type infantry barracks. $810 £360

Victorian model of a butcher's shop, circa 1865. $880 £390

Mid 19th century Bavarian Noah's Ark, 19in. long, complete with animals. $900 £400

A model butcher's shop, circa 1900, 1ft.11in. wide. $1,485 £660

91

MODEL ENGINES

Victorian model of a stationary steam engine.
$190 £85

An old model of a horizontal steam engine. $190 £85

19th century model of a vertical steam engine.
$225 £100

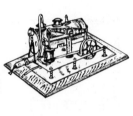

Coll et Cie stationary horizontal steam engine, 33cm. wide, together with a sawbench, 13cm. wide.
$360 £160

'Heinrici' model hot air engine, 18in. high.
$385 £170

Model of a steam Beam engine in glass case. $595 £265

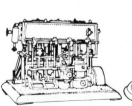

A model of a triple expansion marine steam engine finished in grey and mounted on a chequered baseboard, 10¾in. long. $900 £400

19th century vertical twin-cylinder stationary steam engine in brass and steel, 1ft.3¼in. high, the valve inscribed G. H. Joslin, 1880. $1,125 £500

Model Stuart centre-pillar beam engine, built by R. Wheele, Brighton.
$1,350 £600

92

An automated 'Jolly Nigger' money bank. $70 £30

A late 19th century 'City Bank', 4½in. high. $70 £30

An original cast iron 'standing bear' money box, in two halves, secured from the back with a single screw, 6in. high. $80 £35

A musical tinplate money bank, 4¾in. high, sold with another. $80 £35

Tinplate 'Chocolat Menier' dispenser money box, circa 1920, 10½in. high. $80 £35

Halls patent cast iron money box, dated 1878, 5½in. high. $170 £75

German money box, with presentation inscription. $210 £85

One of two early 20th century cast alloy 'mule' money banks, 4¾in. long. $225 £100

Late 19th century American cat and mouse money box, 8½in. high. $260 £115

Late 19th century American cast iron money bank, 10in. wide. $270 £120

A 20th century English cold painted cast iron 'Stump Speaker' money box, 10in. high.
$295 £130

20th century English cast iron Artillery bank in the form of a cannon, which fires coins into a pill box.
$295 £130

Late 19th century 'Trick Pony' cast iron money bank, 7½in. wide.
$295 £130

Late 19th century jockey and mule money box, 9¾in. long, by James H. Bowen. $305 £135

An American cast iron mechanical money box in the shape of a kneeling Red Indian brave firing a gun at a brown bear.
$360 £160

A cold painted cast iron baseball money box, 9½in. wide. $385 £170

Late 19th century American owl cast iron money bank, 7¾in. high.
$385 £170

A late 19th century American cold painted cast iron money box in the form of a soldier who fires a penny into a tree stump.
$385 £170

94

Late 19th century American 'Uncle Sam' cast iron money box, 11½in. high. $415 £185

A cold painted American cast iron money box 'always did 'spise a mule', 10in. long. $430 £190

Late 19th century American cast iron 'Punch and Judy' money box, 7½in. high. $450 £200

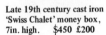

Late 19th century cast iron 'Swiss Chalet' money box, 7in. high. $450 £200

A U.S. iron money bank, depicting Jonah and the Whale, base 10in. long, stamped 'Pat, July 15, 1890'. $450 £200

Late 19th century cast iron 'Organ Bank' money box, 4½in. high. $520 £230

Late 19th century American 'Leap-Frog Bank', 7½in. wide. $620 £275

Late 19th century American monkey and barrel organ cast iron money bank, 6½in. high. $620 £275

A German 'Royal Trick' elephant tinplate mechanical money bank, 6in. long. $1,125 £500

PEDAL CARS

Child's pedal car by Chas. Boardman
& Sons. $250 £145

Austin pedal car, 5ft. long, circa 1950,
English. $360 £160

A child's pedal car, early 1930's.
                    $360 £160

Rare child-sized model of the Austin
Seven racing car. $1,125 £500

PRAMS

English/American wicker-
work pram, 4ft.4in. long,
1930's. $68 £30

A child's folding push-
chair, with light spoke
wheels and rubber tyres,
circa 1900. $100 £45

Victorian pram with fold-
ing hood and brass fittings.
              $100 £45

Victorian bath chair with original frame and handle.
$100 £45

Doll's pram with the original upholstery in black, circa 1860, 24in. high.
$160 £70

A French 'Sociable' child's pram, with wicker basket seat on an iron frame, with large and small wheels.
$180 £80

Late 19th century doll's pram with folding hood.
$190 £85

A Victorian upholstered bathchair.
$250 £110

International Baby Carriage Store child's pushchair, circa 1900, 48in. long.
$325 £130

Edwardian painted wood doll's pushchair with folding hood.
$330 £145

A Victorian baby carriage with brass fittings.
$335 £150

Edwardian doll's perambulator with folding hood and boat-shaped body.
$335 £150

97

SHIPS

Model English galleon made of wood, with cloth sails, circa 1870. $70 £30

A wooden model of a three-masted galleon. $90 £40

Victorian model of a galleon. $90 £40

Wooden model of a clinker-built fishing boat with anchor and oars, 13in. long. $115 £50

Model of a three-masted barquentine surrounded by four small boats, 64cm. wide. $170 £75

Modern large scale wooden model of 'The Mayflower', 150cm. high. $200 £90

A fine 19th century seaman's ship model. $235 £105

A model of a three-masted sailing ship, in a mahogany and glazed case. $270 £120

Two models of three-masted sailing ships, and three other boats, in a glazed display case. $280 £125

Modern model of a French three-masted man-o'-war, 33in. long. $350 £155

A late 19th century wood and canvas model of a barque. $350 £155

A 19th century scale model of a clinker-built sailing boat, 27in. long. $350 £155

Modern English model of H.M.S. Victory, 2ft.5in. long. $385 £170

Late 19th century fully rigged model of H.M.A.P.S. 'Success'. $450 £200

Modern English 1/40 scale model of the Baltimore schooner 'Albatross', 20 x 26in. $675 £300

English model of the French ship 'La Flore', 3ft.9in. high. $675 £300

A model of the 'Cutty Sark'. $700 £310

Mid 19th century model of the galleon 'Elizabeth Jonas', 1ft.5in. wide. $700 £310

A model of the Yarmouth drifter 'Everest', about 1860-75, signed Charles Saunders. $730 £325

Late 19th century model of an American clipper ship, 'Sovereign of the Seas', 3ft.4in. long, 2ft.2in. high. $775 £345

Scale model of a transition period three-masted barque in wood and ivory. $845 £375

19th century model of the clipper 'Nordic', 24in. long. $925 £410

A model of H.M.S. Victory, 40in. long. $970 £430

Early 19th century French prisoner-of-war work 'Man-o'-War', 13in. high. $1,015 £450

 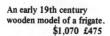  

An early 19th century wooden model of a frigate. $1,070 £475

French prisoner-of-war bone ship model, circa 1800, 10¾in. long. $1,350 £625

An English bone and wood model of a clipper ship, 1ft.4in. wide, circa 1860. $1,465 £650

A French prisoner-of-war bone model of a galleon, 14in. long. $1,755 £780

A Napoleonic period, sailor made, ivory model of a three-masted frigate, 9½in. long. $2,140 £950

French prisoner-of-war bone ship model, circa 1800, 8¾in. long. $2,140 £950

Boxwood model of a seventy-six gun, English Ship of the line, 10in. high, 14in. long. $2,475 £1,100

The frigate 'Mars', a full rigged, pinned bone model ship, 19½in. long. $2,475 £1,100

French prisoner-of-war bone model of the 'Temeraire, 19in. long. $2,700 £1,200

A Napoleonic prisoner-of-war bone model of a ship. $2,700 £1,200

French prisoner-of-war bone ship model, circa 1800, 14½in. long. $2,810 £1,250

Model of the three-masted ship 'Countess Margaret', 4ft. long. $2,925 £1,300

Fully rigged model of the seventy-four gun man-o'-war 'Royal George', 1782.
$2,925 £1,300

Early 20th century bone and wood model of a French man-o'-war, 12 x 10in.
$3,150 £1,400

French prisoner-of-war model of the frigate 'Venus', circa 1815.
$3,150 £1,400

Model of an eighty-four gun man-o'-war, 8½in. long.
$3,825 £1,700

English man-o'-war model ship, circa 1815, in excellent condition, 58in. long.
$4,500 £2,000

A French prisoner-of-war boxwood ship model, 14in. long, circa 1800-10.
$5,175 £2,300

A bone and ivory prisoner-of war model of a man-o'-war, 16in. long.
$5,625 £2,500

Prisoner-of-war bone model of H.M.S. Mars.
$6,190 £2,750

Boxwood, ebony and copper sheathed model of a frigate. $6,750 £3,000

A French prisoner-of-war bone ship model, 13in. long, circa 1800.
$7,315 £3,250

Contemporary prisoner-of-war fully rigged bone and ebony model of H.M. 16-gun brig 'Pelican', 20in. wide. $7,735 £3,500

Bone model of H.M.S. Union, 44in. long.
$7,875 £3,500

Bone, horn and hair model of a French ship, circa 1800-10, 76cm. long.
$8,440 £3,750

Early 19th century box-wood and ebony copper sheathed model of 'Le Heros'. $9,450 £4,200

Bone prisoner-of-war model of a three-masted man-o'-war. $11,250 £5,000

French prisoner-of-war bone model of a man-o'-war, early 19th century, 91cm. long. $13,500 £6,000

Set of ship models of the commands of Captain Purvis, in their original glazed walnut display cabinet.
$29,250 £13,000

A model of a seventy-two gun man-o'-war, circa 1740, 57in. long.
$33,750 £15,000

Clockwork pirate ship, made in Japan in
1950, with firing cannons, 12in. long.
$70 £30

Tinplate clockwork model ship, 9¼in.
long, circa 1915-20. $100 £45

Clockwork battleship 'Dreadnought',
8in. long, 1920-25. $250 £110

An early tinplate Bing clockwork torpedo
boat, 1ft.10in. long, circa 1910. $295 £130

German tinplate clockwork paddle boat
'Glasgow', 13in. long. $565 £250

Tinplate four-funnelled battleship,
probably by Bing, circa 1912, 1ft.
5in. long. $865 £385

Clockwork boat on wheels. $945 £420

Tinplate clockwork battleship by Ernst
Plank, circa 1903. $2,700 £1,200

Modern wood model of a trawler, 32in. long, with radio controlled motor.
$100 £45

Working model of a screw driven Edwardian steam yacht, 49in. long.
$280 £125

Victorian model of a paddle steamer, 37in. long.
$340 £150

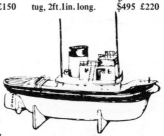

A Basset-Lowke working model of a tug, 2ft.1in. long.
$495 £220

19th century working model of a tug boat, complete with 50cc petrol engine.
$630 £280

A well made steam powered model Thames tug, 58in. long. $700 £310

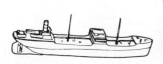

A Bassett-Lowke working model of a tanker, 2ft.5in. wide.
$700 £310

Scale model of the S.S. Durley Chine.
$730 £325

Mid 20th century working model of a
destroyer, 5ft.6in. long. $790 £350

Ship builder's scale model, 37in. long.
$790 £350

Scale half model of the steel twin-
screw steamer 'Winifred', 116cm. long.
$820 £360

Walnut cased model of a herring trawler,
circa 1890. $865 £385

Unusual spirit-fired live steam launch,
18¼in. long. $900 £400

Dockyard model of a tug boat, with
brass fittings, 44in. long. $935 £415

A large scale model of a steam tug,
in full working order. $1,080 £480

Mappin & Webb model silver motor
launch, 1965, 45.7cm. long.
$1,410 £625

Mid 20th century English half-block model of the tanker 'Bilswood', in a stained oak glazed case, 8ft.5in. long. $1,520 £675

A half-block model of the steamer 'Twingone', 6ft.7in. long.
$1,575 £700

A Georgian diorama of a naval dockyard scene, inscribed 'Built by Robert Tilgour Dundee 1817', 43in. wide. $1,800 £800

A shipbuilder's large model of the 'R.M.S. Orcades', 8ft. long.
$2,250 £1,000

A shipbuilder's model of the steamer 'S.S. Hookwood', 6ft. long.
$2,475 £1,100

Builder's model of a Blackwall frigate, 1837. $2,700 £1,200

A live steam exhibition model of an ocean-going tug 'Margaret', 4ft.8in. long, circa 1938-42. $3,150 £1,400

A dockyard model of R.F.A. Celerol, 'Dazzle-camouflaged', World War I style. $4,500 £2,000

THEATRES

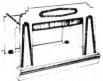

A child's toy theatre, with theatre seats and appointments. $70 £30

A living marionette theatre complete with thirteen puppets. $80 £35

Mid 19th century German toy theatre. $260 £115

Late 19th century Guignol theatre, 81cm. high. $325 £145

Victorian toy theatre showing a sewing class in progress. $880 £390

A Victorian penny-in-the-slot walnut musical cabinet in the form of a theatre. $1,295 £575

Part of a complete early 20th century Indonesian puppet theatre. $1,745 £775

A Meccano display model of a showman's traction engine, 2ft.5½in. long.
$200 £90

Model of a traction engine. $865 £385

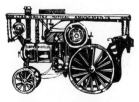

Model steam engine. $1,575 £700

Scale model of a road haulage traction
engine, 2ft.3in. long. $1,800 £800

Fine 2in. scale live steam coal-fired
model Allchin agricultural traction
engine, finished in red and black,
26in. $3,375 £1,500

Model steam fairground traction
engine. $3,375 £1,500

3in. scale traction engine. $4,050 £1,800

Burrell traction engine model, 3in.
scale, in full working order.
$7,315 £3,250

TRAINS

A 2-2-0 live steam model engine with whistle and try-cock at front of the boiler, 7¼in. $115 £50

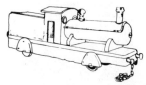

Unmechanical train, painted in green and red. $135 £60

A gauge 1, 0-4-4 model, solidly built steam engine of the North Eastern Falls. $250 £110

'Dragon', a 2-2-2 live steam engine with whistle and twin oscillating cylinders, 9in. $250 £110

A 2-2-0 live steam model engine with whistle, filler plug, main steam valve and try-cock at the front of the boiler, 7in. $250 £110

A well constructed brass model steam engine, 12½in. by 7in. high, complete with moving levers. $260 £115

Cast metal 'HO' gauge two-rail electric model of the Italian Railways Express diesel car by Conti. $270 £120

A Victorian coal-fired model steam engine, 13½in. high. $280 £125

A 2-2-0 live steam model engine with filler
valve and dome, twin oscillating cylinders,
7in. $280 £125

Early spirit-fired brass 'Piddler' engine,
mid 19th century, 9in. long.$300 £135

19th century 4½in. gauge brass and copper
live steam coal-fired engine, 1ft.5½in. long.
                                        $640 £285

3½in. gauge Adams saddle tank locomotive, sold with tracks. $675 £300

Mid 19th century working model
railway 2-4-0 steam engine with
detachable methylated spirit three-
wick burner, 13in. long. $700 £310

Live steam coal-fired 3½in. gauge 0-4-0
'Tich' tank engine, 15½in. long.
                                        $745 £330

Fine gauge 1 live steam spirit-fired 0-2-2-0
side tank locomotive complete with pot
boiler, by Bing. $855 £380

Early Bing gauge 'O' live steam tank
engine no. 3410. $865 £385

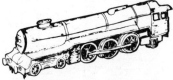

A well made 3½in. gauge 4-6-2 Pacific class working model loco of 'The Hielan Lassie', 36in. long. $965 £430

Tinplate reversing engine 'London' by Mathias Hess, circa 1885, in original box.
$990 £440

7mm. scale three-rail electric model of a London and North Eastern Railway Class N2 side tank locomotive, 10½in. long.
$1,080 £480

3½in. gauge locomotive 'Hackfly'.
$1,080 £480

Gauge 'O' Bassett-Lowke 'Flying Scotsman' locomotive and tender. $1,195 £530

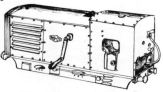

A well made working model of a diesel shunting engine, 31½in. long.
$1,225 £545

3½in. gauge model train sold with drivers flat seated truck for garden running. $1,225 £545

Early live steam locomotive, 3¼in. gauge, circa 1880. $1,350 £600

112

A 4½in. gauge scale model of a
coal-fired locomotive 'Jimpy'.
$1,375 £610

Early 20th century 2½in. gauge spirit-fired model
of a Great Central Railway Robinson Class
Express side tank locomotive by Bassett-Lowke,
21½in. long. $1,465 £650

Marklin gauge '1' clockwork tank locomotive, circa 1915, 1ft.5in. long.
$1,530 £680

Steam model of a four coupled
tank engine, 3½in. gauge.
$1,555 £690

2½in. gauge live steam coal-fired 4-6-2
locomotive 'Saint Lawrence' with
tender, 3ft.8in. long. $1,755 £780

Steam model locomotive of the
Great Western Railway.
$2,700 £1,200

Carette live steam spirit-fired 4-4-0
locomotive with cast iron frames
13½in., lacking tender.
$3,150 £1,400

5in. gauge model of the 0-4-0 Hunslet
'Alice' saddle tank quarry locomotive
'Aileen', 33in. long. $4,275 £1,900

113

Hand built 'O' gauge electric 2-6-4
LMS tank locomotive, 33cm. long.
$115 £50

Hand built 4-6-0 gauge 'O' electric
locomotive and tender, 41cm. long.
$170 £75

A Bassett-Lowke 'O' gauge clockwork
'Duke of York' 4-4-0 locomotive and
tender, 37.5cm. long overall.
$200 £90

Good German clockwork locomotive
'Mercury', 1ft.4½in. long. $395 £175

Gauge '1' Carette live steam spirit-
fired 2-2-0 locomotive, circa 1910,
1ft.3in. long. $405 £180

'O' gauge model of the 'Duchess of
Montrose' locomotive. $450 £200

Bassett-Lowke 'O' gauge model of the
'Flying Scotsman'. $565 £250

Mint condition Hornby gauge 'O' electric locomotive, 1ft.3in. long.
$700 £310

Gauge 'O' Bassett-Lowke 'Royal Scot' electric locomotive and tender.
$745 £330

A German gauge '1' live steam spirit-fired reversing locomotive, 1ft.6½in. long.
$745 £330

German 2½in. gauge '3' live steam spirit-fired locomotive, 1ft.6in. long.
$765 £340

An 'O' gauge model of an A3 Pacific 4-6-2 steam locomotive. $900 £400

Bassett-Lowke 'O' gauge electric 4-6-2 'Princess Royal' locomotive and tender, 51cm. long. $990 £440

3½in. gauge working model of a 4-4-0 Trans-American locomotive and tender. $1,070 £475

Model of an LNWR locomotive and tender, 15in. long overall.
$1,070 £475

7¼in. gauge electric display model of Delaware Lackawana & Western 4-4-0 locomotive. $1,125 £500

A coal fired working model of the
LMS locomotive 'Highland Chief'.
$1,240 £550

Atlantic type 4-4-2 steam locomotive
and tender, 1½in. gauge coal fired
full working model, by H. Bell, circa
1930, 33in. long. $1,465 £650

Gauge 'O' three-rail electric model of
the 'Royal Scot' by Bassett-Lowke.
$1,465 £650

7mm. finescale two-rail electric model
of a Midland Railway Johnstone 2-4-0
locomotive and tender, 14in. long.
$1,800 £800

2½in. gauge model of the Great Western
Railway 4-6-0 locomotive and tender
'Purley Grange', 1937, 34in. long.
$1,915 £850

2½in. gauge spirit-fired model of a
4-4-2 locomotive and tender by
Bassett-Lowke, 29½in. long.
$2,140 £950

'Heilan Lassie', 3½in. gauge model
locomotive. $2,230 £990

A model of a Midland Railway compound 4-4-0 locomotive and tender,
with a full-brazed riveted super-
heated copper boiler, 5ft. long.
$2,250 £1,000

A Bing 4-2-2 live steam spirit-fired
locomotive and tender, sold with
several coaches. $2,530 £1,125

A Bing spirit-fired 4-4-0 locomotive
in apple green livery, 22½in. long.
$2,700 £1,200

Model of a North Eastern 1849
type Kitson Thompson and
Hewitson, Leeds, 2-4-0 locomotive.
$2,810 £1,250

Carette North Eastern spirit-fired
locomotive, circa 1905.
$3,375 £1,500

Fine 2½in. gauge model of
Stephenson's 'Rocket',
built by A. Tyrer, Hastings,
11½in. long. $3,375 £1,500

Gauge 'O' live steam spirit-fired model of an
American 2-8-0 locomotive and tender,
built by A. Beale, Chelmsford, 1954, 17in.
long. $3,600 £1,600

A 5in. gauge model of the Adams 4-4-0
locomotive and tender No. 563 built
by H. W. Webb, Stoke D'Abernon, about
5ft. long. $3,600 £1,600

Working model of the Great Northern
locomotive No. 7 'Scorpion', overall
length 170cm. $4,500 £2,000

TRAINS AND TENDER

A 5in. gauge model of the Class T9 locomotive and eight-wheeled tender, built by B. Mount in 1967.　　　　　　　　　$4,500　£2,000

Marklin gauge '1' live steam fired locomotive 'The Great Bear', 2ft.5in. long, circa 1910.　　　　　　　　　$6,190　£2,750

A 3½in. gauge working steam model of a Duchess Class locomotive and tender in maroon livery of LMS.　　　　　　$6,750　£3,000

The 'Super Claud' model locomotive, 5in. gauge.　　$7,425　£3,300

A 5in. gauge working scale model of Beyer Peqcock Rhodesian railway locomotive, 6ft. long.　　　　　　　$7,875　£3,500

Bing gauge 'O' clockwork train set. $190 £85

Gauge 'O' clockwork 4-4-0 locomotive no. 1924, sold with tender and coach, circa 1920. $225 £100

Rare tinplate French carpet toy train, 15in. long, circa 1870. $235 £105

Issmayer gauge 'O' clockwork train set, late 1920's. $250 £110

Bing gauge 'OO' clockwork miniature table railway, sold with various coaches and rails, in original box, circa 1920. $290 £130

119

TRAINS WITH CARRIAGES

Early German gauge 'O' model railway collection. $290 £130

Carl Bub electric model railway in original box. $325 £145

Bing tinplate gauge 'OO' table railway, circa 1920. $325 £145

'O' gauge clockwork train set by Louis Marx. $335 £150

A clockwork Ernst Plank 2-2-0 engine and tender with key, circa 1905, sold with three four-wheeled coaches.
$450 £200

Unusual 2½in. gauge static model of an SNCF diesel electric panoramic rail-car, 4ft.7in. long. $620 £275

Early tinplate carpet toy train and carriages, French, circa 1880, 1ft.7in. long. $620 £275

Early gauge '3' Ernst Plank live steam boxed train set, circa 1905. $640 £285

Part of a Lionel gauge 'O' model railway collection. $720 £320

Cast metal 'HO' gauge two-rail electric model of the Italian Railways three coach train set 'Il Settebello' by Conti. $855 £380

TRAINS WITH CARRIAGES

'OO' gauge clockwork train set complete with rolling stock. $900 £400

Early Marklin gauge '1' clockwork locomotive, 12in. long. $1,125 £500

Bing centre rail electric 4-4-2 locomotive and tender, sold with several coaches.
$1,575 £700

Marklin clockwork 'precursor' 4-4-2 tank locomotive, 16¼in., sold with three
coaches. $1,800 £800

Part of a collection of gauge '1' three-rail electric Continental railway rolling
stock by Marklin. $1,800 £800

Bassett-Lowke gauge 'O' L.M.S. 12-wheeled dining car.   **$110 £55**

Locomotive engineering works 2-4-0 valve gear demonstration chassis, 4ft. 2in. long, circa 1900.   **$217 £115**

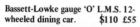

Two gauge '1' bogie passenger coaches by Carette for Bassett-Lowke, 1ft.4½in. long.   **$218 £110**

Gunthermann tinplate tram-car, circa 1925-30, 10in. long.   **$260 £135**

Part of a Max Handwerk gauge 'O' clockwork train, circa 1930.   **$315 £140**

Early Bing gauge '1' GNR bogie passenger coach, 1ft.1½in. long, circa 1915.   **$435 £220**

Marklin gauge '1' bogie CIWR sleeping car, circa 1919, 1ft.8¾in. long.   **$870 £440**

TRAIN DISPLAY

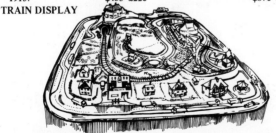

Fine electric hand built working model railway exhibition display, circa 1947, 12ft. x 15ft.6in.   **$4,050 £1,800**

INDEX

125